Map Skills

Dr. Bernard A. Fox

Illustrated by Gloria McKeown and Laurie Conley

To the Student

Maps and globes are your guides to the world. They present all sorts of useful information in a clear, simple way. With a map or globe, you can find out where places are and how far apart they are. You can discover what a place is like—hilly or flat, hot or cold, wet or dry. You can learn different facts about our Earth—where the most people live, which crops a country grows, where oil can be found. Then, of course, there are the kinds of maps you can use every day—the bus map that helps you get around town and the road map you use on vacation.

Reading maps and globes isn't difficult, but you do need to understand certain things about what they are telling you. *Map Skills* explains those things and gives you a chance to practice them. When you have finished this book, you'll have the skills you need to use these two important tools.

ISBN 978-0-8454-9899-6
Copyright © 2004 The Continental Press, Inc.

Table of Contents

Using the Key, Direction Finder, and Scale

There are many kinds of maps. A map can show countries and cities, roads and distances, bodies of land and water, and so on. A map can also give information about weather, climate, products, population, transportation, elevation, history, or almost anything else.

To use a map, you have to understand what it is telling you. These parts of the map will help you read it.

Title: This tells you what the map shows.

Key: This explains the symbols used on the map.

Direction Finder: This shows you the orientation of the map—which way is north, and so on.

Scale of Distance: This tells what the distances on the map are equal to on the ground. Distances may be measured in feet, miles, meters, or kilometers.

Study this map. Then circle T for True or F for False for each statement below.

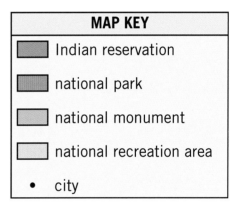

ARIZONA
Major National Parks, Monuments,
Recreation Areas, and Indian Reservations

MAP KEY

Indian reservation

national park

national monument

national recreation area

• city

Scale

0   50   100   150   200
miles

T	F	**1.** The state shown on the map is Arizona.
T	F	**2.** Yuma is the name of an Indian reservation.
T	F	**3.** Tohono O'odham is the name of a national park.
T	F	**4.** Saguaro is the name of a national park.
T	F	**5.** Petrified Forest National Park is south of the Navajo Indian Reservation.
T	F	**6.** Phoenix is north of the Gila River Indian Reservation.
T	F	**7.** Grand Canyon National Park is northeast of the Fort Apache Indian Reservation.
T	F	**8.** Tucson is southeast of Lake Mead National Recreation Area.
T	F	**9.** From Phoenix to Tucson is about 100 miles.
T	F	**10.** From Yuma to Phoenix is about 250 miles.

Using a Grid on a Street Map

To help you find places you are looking for, most maps have a **grid.** The grid divides the map into small spaces. Letters name the spaces from top to bottom, and numbers name the spaces from side to side. The location of any place on the map can be described by putting a letter and a number together. For example, on the map of part of New York City below, Pennsylvania Station is in space E-2. To find it, you look across the spaces marked E and down the spaces marked 2. Do this and circle the station.

Now find and number these places on the map.

1. Madison Square Park F-3

2. United Nations D-4

3. Carnegie Hall B-2, B-3

4. Rockefeller Center C-3

5. Empire State Building E-3

6. Lincoln Center A-2

7. Times Square D-2

8. Hunter College A-4

9. Lincoln Tunnel D-1

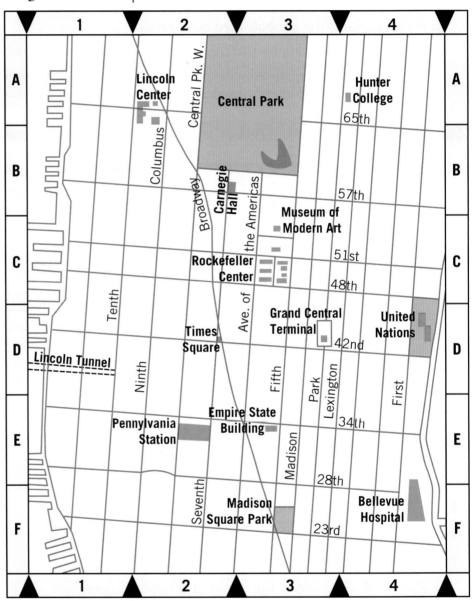

Study the map and its grid to answer these questions.

10. In what grid space is Grand Central Terminal? _____

11. In what grid space is the Museum of Modern Art? _____

12. In what two grid spaces is Bellevue Hospital? _____

13. In what four grid spaces is Central Park? _____

Using a Grid on a Map

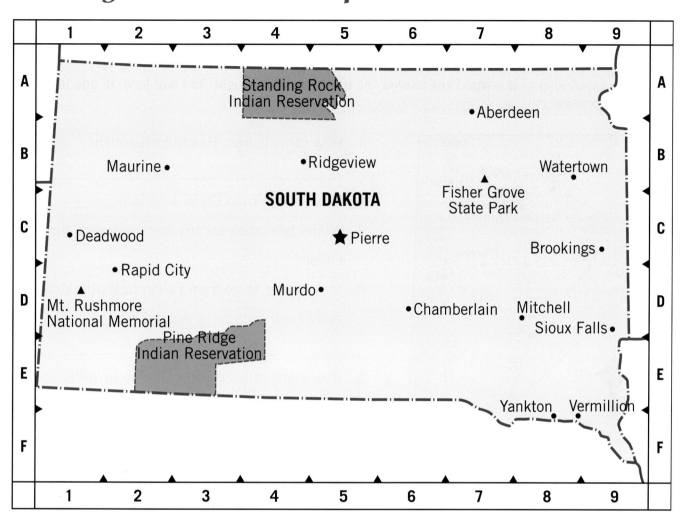

Study this map of South Dakota. Then use the grid to answer the questions below.

1. What town is shown in grid space A-7? _____

2. What town is shown in grid space C-1? _____

3. What town is shown in grid space B-4? _____

4. What tourist attraction is shown in grid space D-1? _____

5. What two towns are shown in grid space F-8? _____

6. In what grid space is the state capital, Pierre? _____

7. In what grid spaces are the following towns? Murdo _____ Maurine _____

   Rapid City _____ Brookings _____

8. In what grid space is Fisher Grove State Park? _____

9. In what five grid spaces is the Pine Ridge Indian Reservation? _____

10. In what two grid spaces is the Standing Rock Indian Reservation? _____

Using Mileage Markers and Mileage Tables

Road maps show you how to get from one place to another. They also show the distance between places. Look at the map below. The number of miles between the cities is printed along the roads.

Study this road map of Nevada. Then answer the questions at the right. You will have to add to find some of the answers.

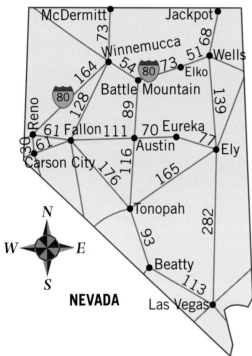

1. How far is it from Beatty to Tonopah? _____

   _____

2. How far is it from Ely to Jackpot? _____

3. Which two cities are the same distance from

   Fallon? _____

4. Is it shorter to go from Fallon to Battle Mountain

   by Winnemucca or by Austin? _____

   _____

5. How many miles is it from Reno to Wells on

   Highway 80? _____

To help you find the distances between larger cities, some maps also have a **mileage table.** On the left side of the table, you look for the city you are starting out from. On the top of the table, you look for the city you are going to. Where the lines for the two cities meet, the table shows the distance between them. For example, to find the distance between Ely and Elko, look across the Ely line and down the Elko line. You will see that these cities are 190 miles apart.

	Carson City	Elko	Ely	Fallon	Las Vegas	Reno	Winnemucca
Carson City		316	319	61	443	30	189
Elko	316		190	255	472	291	127
Ely	319	190		258	282	319	290
Fallon	61	255	258		382	61	128
Las Vegas	443	472	282	382		443	465
Reno	30	291	319	61	443		164
Winnemucca	189	127	290	128	465	164	

Study the mileage table. Then complete the sentences below. You will have to subtract to find some of the answers.

6. It is _____ miles from Carson City to Las Vegas.

7. It is _____ miles from Fallon to Ely.

8. It is _____ miles from Elko to Carson City.

9. Winnemucca is _____ miles farther from Las Vegas than it is from Elko.

Using What You Have Learned

Study this map and the mileage chart that shows the distances between some of the cities on the map. Then complete the sentences below.

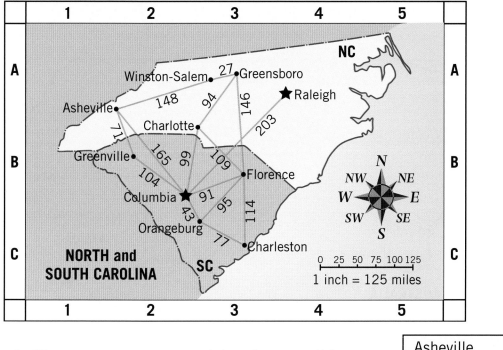

	Asheville	Charleston	Columbia	Florence	Greensboro
Asheville		285	165	256	175
Charleston	285		120	114	260
Columbia	165	120		91	193
Florence	256	114	91		146
Greensboro	175	260	193	146	

1. There are _____ states shown on this map.

2. Columbia is _____ miles _____ of Charlotte.

3. Winston-Salem is _____ miles _____ of Greensboro.

4. On this map, two inches stands for _____ miles.

5. The capital of North Carolina is _____.

6. The capital of South Carolina is _____.

7. The two cities located in grid space B-2 are _____ and
   _____.

8. The two cities located in grid space A-3 are _____ and
   _____.

9. Columbia is _____ miles from Greensboro.

10. Florence is _____ miles from Asheville.

11. Charleston is _____ miles farther from Florence than it is from Orangeburg.

12. The shortest route from Charleston to Asheville is _____ miles long.

Understanding and Using Political Maps

Political means "having to do with government."
A **political map** shows areas under different
governments. It shows the boundary lines
between countries, states, provinces,
counties, and so on. A political
map usually also shows cities,
especially the capitals where
the governments of the
areas are located.

**Study this political map.
Then complete the
activities below.**

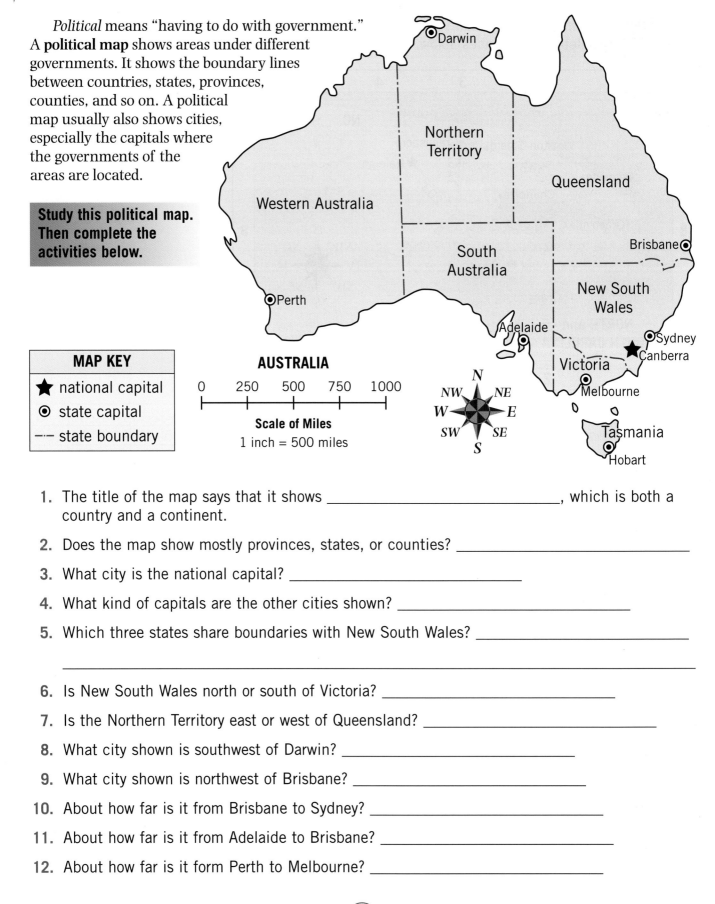

MAP KEY
★ national capital
⊙ state capital
--- state boundary

AUSTRALIA

Scale of Miles
1 inch = 500 miles

1. The title of the map says that it shows _____, which is both a country and a continent.

2. Does the map show mostly provinces, states, or counties? _____

3. What city is the national capital? _____

4. What kind of capitals are the other cities shown? _____

5. Which three states share boundaries with New South Wales? _____

   _____

6. Is New South Wales north or south of Victoria? _____

7. Is the Northern Territory east or west of Queensland? _____

8. What city shown is southwest of Darwin? _____

9. What city shown is northwest of Brisbane? _____

10. About how far is it from Brisbane to Sydney? _____

11. About how far is it from Adelaide to Brisbane? _____

12. About how far is it form Perth to Melbourne? _____

8

Recognizing That Boundaries Change

Political maps change because governments and countries change. In 1989, changes took place in Eastern Europe that resulted in the fall of Communist governments there. Several countries, including the Soviet Union, broke up into smaller countries. In 2003, Yugoslavia also broke into smaller countries.

Study the two maps below. Then answer the questions.

MAP A

Eastern Europe, 1989

MAP B

Eastern Europe, 2003

1. Croatia was part of what country? _____

2. Identify three small countries near the coast that used to be part of the Soviet Union.

   _____

3. Name a country that split both the country and its name into two different countries.

   _____

4. Ukraine was part of what country? _____

5. What country on Map A was reunited with its western half? _____

6. What countries border Belarus? _____

7. Which of the following countries is shown the same on both maps: Russia, Yugoslavia, or

   Romania? _____

Recognizing Bodies of Land and Water

Maps can show the different bodies of land and water on Earth.

- A **continent** is the largest body of land. There are seven continents: Africa, Antarctica, Asia, Australia, Europe, North America, and South America.

- A **peninsula** is a body of land that is surrounded by water on three sides.

- An **isthmus** is a narrow strip of land that connects two larger areas of land.

- An **ocean** is the largest body of water. There are four main oceans: Arctic, Atlantic, Indian, and Pacific.

- A **sea** is smaller than an ocean and is at least partly surrounded by land.

- A **gulf** is another large body of water, reaching into land from an ocean or sea.

- A **lake** is a body of water completely surrounded by land.

- A **river** is a long body of water that flows along a certain path.

Study the map below. Complete each map label with the name of a body of land or water: continent, peninsula, isthmus, ocean, sea, gulf, lake, or river.

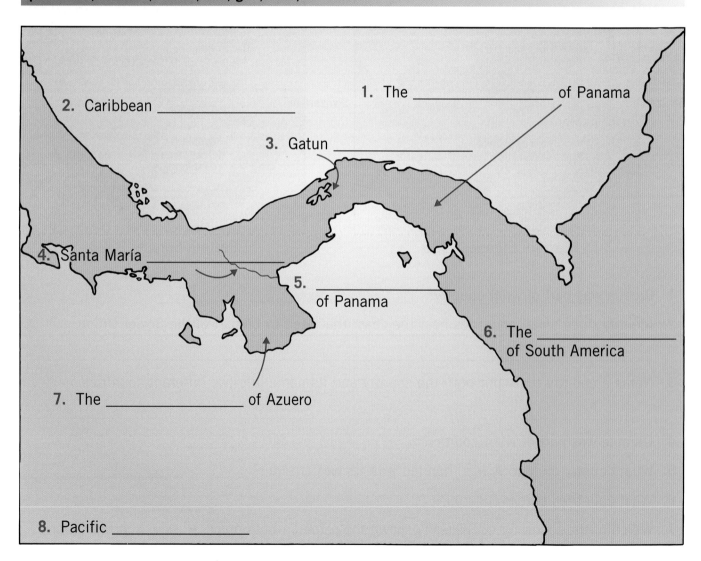

1. The _____ of Panama

2. Caribbean _____

3. Gatun _____

4. Santa María _____

5. _____ of Panama

6. The _____ of South America

7. The _____ of Azuero

8. Pacific _____

Recognizing Bodies of Land and Water

Here are some more bodies of land and water that you should know.

- A **cape** is like a peninsula only smaller and more pointed.
- An **island** is a body of land completely surrounded by water.
- An **archipelago** is a group of islands.
- A **bay** is like a gulf only much smaller.
- A **strait** is a narrow body of water that connects two larger bodies of water.
- A **tributary** is a river that runs into a larger river.

Study the map of Japan. Complete each map label with the name of a body of land or water: cape, island, bay, or strait. Then circle the answer to each question below.

9. What is Japan?

   a. an island

   b. a continent

   c. an archipelago

10. How many tributaries does the Tone River have?

    a. none   b. one   c. two

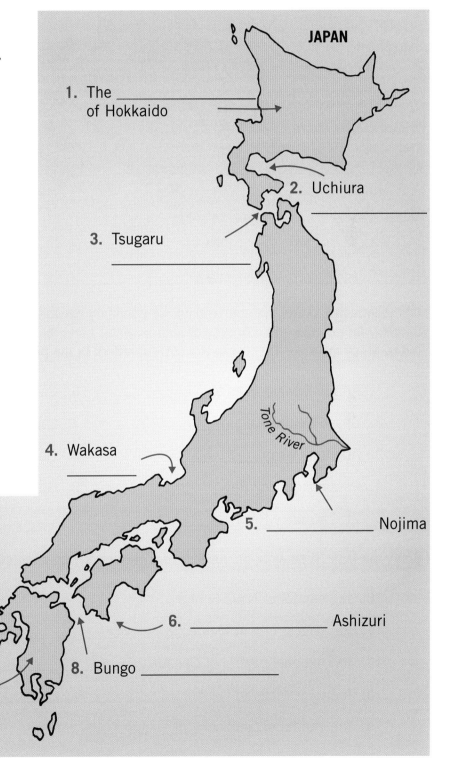

JAPAN

1. The _____ of Hokkaido

2. Uchiura _____

3. Tsugaru _____

4. Wakasa _____

5. _____ Nojima

6. _____ Ashizuri

7. The _____ of Kyushu

8. Bungo _____

Tone River

Using What You Have Learned

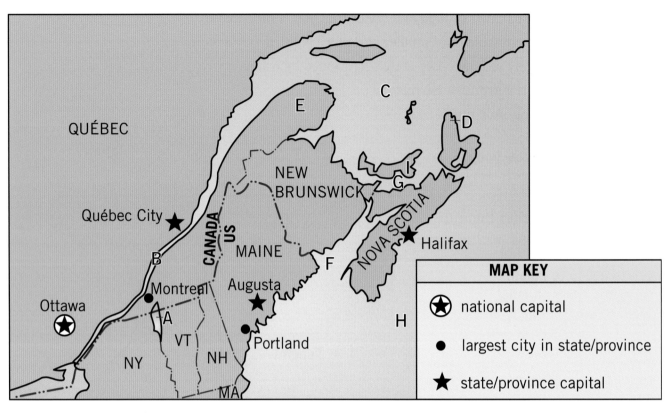

The map above shows the area around the boundary between the northeastern United States and Canada. An example of each body of land or water listed below is marked on the map with a capital letter. Study the map. Then write the correct letters in the blanks.

1. Prince Edward Island _____

2. Gaspé Peninsula _____

3. Atlantic Ocean _____

4. Passamaquoddy Bay _____

5. St. Lawrence River _____

6. Cape North _____

7. Lake Champlain _____

8. Northumberland Strait _____

9. Gulf of St. Lawrence _____

Study the map. Then write the name of the correct city on each blank below.

10. the capital of Nova Scotia _____

11. the largest city in Maine _____

12. the national capital of Canada _____

13. the largest city in Québec _____

14. the capital of Québec _____

Understanding Topographic Maps

Topographic maps show the elevation of an area, or how high it is above sea level. They may use shadings, colors, lines, or other symbols to do this. The topographic map below uses **contour lines** and colors to show elevation.

The lines and colors mark areas where the elevation changes by 100 feet. A topographic map may also show natural features, such as rivers, as well as other features, such as roads.

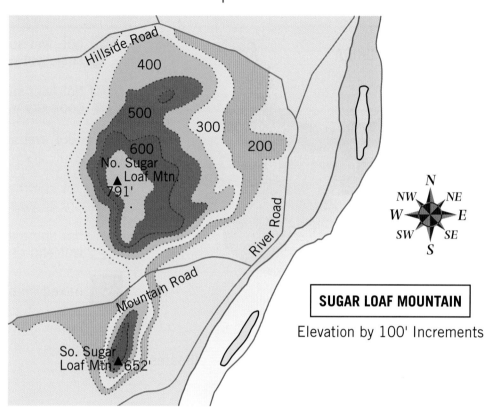

SUGAR LOAF MOUNTAIN

Elevation by 100' Increments

Study the topographic map and its key. Then answer the questions below.

1. What area does the map show? _____

2. What three roads are shown on the map? _____

3. How high is the peak north of Mountain Road? _____

4. How high is the peak south of Mountain Road? _____

5. What are the other five elevation heights marked with contour lines on this map?

   _____

6. How high is the mountain at the point where it is closest to River Road?

   _____

7. What is the highest elevation that Mountain Road crosses? _____

8. Is the elevation higher near River Road or near Hillside Road? _____

   _____

13

Understanding Climate Maps

Climate maps show the kind of weather a region has over many years.

Study the climate map of China. Then circle T (true) or F (false) for each statement below.

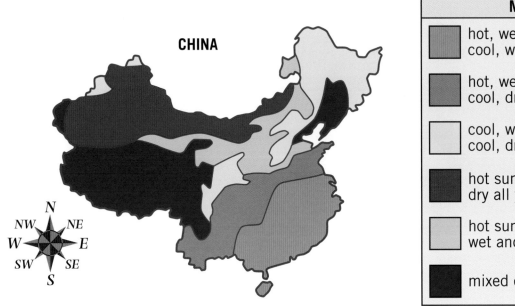

CHINA

MAP KEY

hot, wet summer;
cool, wet winter

hot, wet summer;
cool, dry winter

cool, wet summer;
cool, dry winter

hot summer; cool winter;
dry all year round

hot summer; cool winter;
wet and dry all year round

mixed climates

T   F   **1.** Eastern China has three kinds of climates.

T   F   **2.** It never rains in China.

T   F   **3.** Southeastern China has cool, wet winters.

T   F   **4.** Most of northwestern China has hot, dry summers.

T   F   **5.** Most of China has cool winters.

T   F   **6.** The westernmost part of China has a mixed climate.

T   F   **7.** The northeasternmost part of China has hot, wet summers and cool, wet winters.

T   F   **8.** A part of China that stretches from southwest to northeast has hot, wet summers and cool, dry winters.

T   F   **9.** China has six different types of climate.

T   F   **10.** An island off the southeastern coast of China has mixed climates.

Understanding Rainfall Maps

Rainfall maps show the average amount of rain that falls in a year in an area.

Study this rainfall map. Then circle T (true) or F (false) for each statement below.

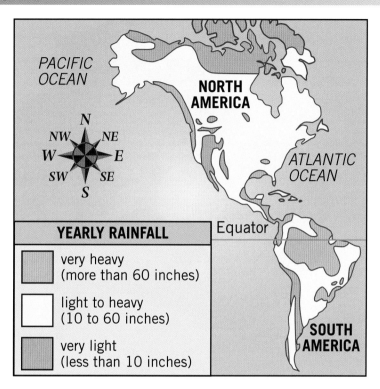

T   F   **1.** Most of North America has very heavy rainfall.

T   F   **2.** Most of South America has very light rainfall.

T   F   **3.** Many areas along the equator have very heavy rainfall.

T   F   **4.** The northernmost part of North America has very light rainfall.

T   F   **5.** Much of the southwestern part of the United States is dry.

T   F   **6.** South America has areas of very light rain on both coasts.

T   F   **7.** The eastern coast of Central America has very heavy rainfall.

T   F   **8.** A portion of the Pacific coast of Canada and the United States has very heavy rainfall.

T   F   **9.** The western coast of most of Central America has very heavy rainfall.

T   F   **10.** The easternmost tip of South America has very heavy rainfall.

Understanding Vegetation Maps

Vegetation maps show the plant life of a region.

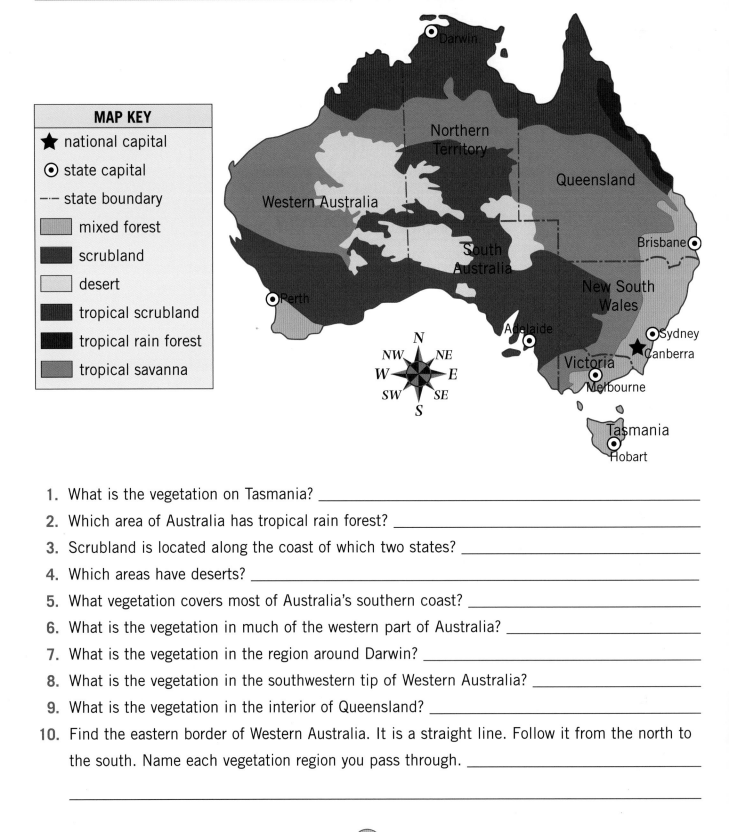

1. What is the vegetation on Tasmania? _____

2. Which area of Australia has tropical rain forest? _____

3. Scrubland is located along the coast of which two states? _____

4. Which areas have deserts? _____

5. What vegetation covers most of Australia's southern coast? _____

6. What is the vegetation in much of the western part of Australia? _____

7. What is the vegetation in the region around Darwin? _____

8. What is the vegetation in the southwestern tip of Western Australia? _____

9. What is the vegetation in the interior of Queensland? _____

10. Find the eastern border of Western Australia. It is a straight line. Follow it from the north to the south. Name each vegetation region you pass through. _____

_____

Understanding Land Use Maps

Land use maps show where things are grown, raised, mined, or made in an area.

Study this land use map. Then circle T (true) or F (false) for each statement below.

	FARM PRODUCTS OF NORWAY, SWEDEN, FINLAND		
	cattle		oats
	sheep		rye
	reindeer		wheat

T   F   **1.** Cattle are raised in Norway, Sweden, and Finland.

T   F   **2.** Wheat is grown in Norway.

T   F   **3.** Reindeer are raised in Sweden.

T   F   **4.** Oats are grown in Finland.

T   F   **5.** Sheep are raised in Sweden and Finland.

T   F   **6.** Rye is grown in Finland and Sweden but not in Norway.

T   F   **7.** Cattle are raised in the northern parts of Finland and Norway.

T   F   **8.** Wheat is grown in southern Sweden and Finland.

T   F   **9.** Rye is grown along the southern coast of Sweden.

T   F   **10.** Reindeer are raised in northern Norway.

T   F   **11.** The only product raised in all three countries is wheat.

T   F   **12.** Norway's major farm products are grains.

Using What You Have Learned

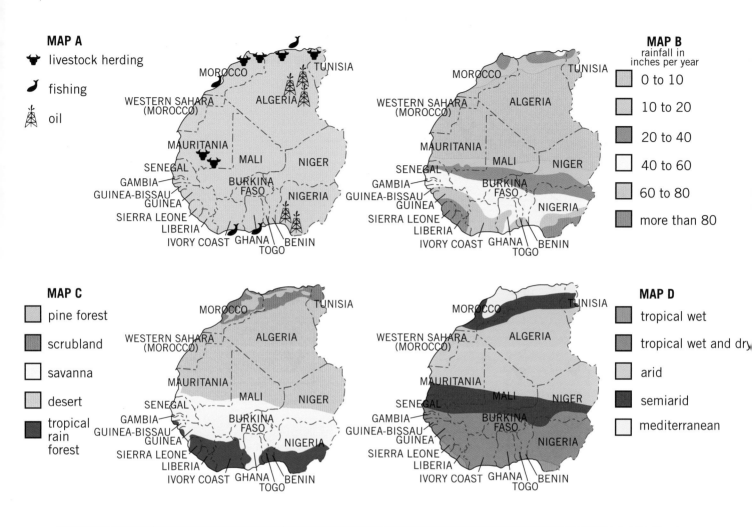

MAP A
- 🐂 livestock herding
- 🐟 fishing
- ⛽ oil

MAP B
rainfall in inches per year
- 0 to 10
- 10 to 20
- 20 to 40
- 40 to 60
- 60 to 80
- more than 80

MAP C
- pine forest
- scrubland
- savanna
- desert
- tropical rain forest

MAP D
- tropical wet
- tropical wet and dry
- arid
- semiarid
- mediterranean

Study these four maps of western Africa. Then answer the questions below.

1. What kind of map is each of the maps shown?

   A _____   C _____

   B _____   D _____

2. What is the largest climate region shown? _____

3. What is the largest vegetation region shown? _____

4. What is the main land use in the northernmost part of western Africa? _____

5. Which country has more rainfall on the whole, Nigeria or Mauritania? _____

6. In which two countries is oil found? _____

7. How much rainfall does the largest rainfall region receive? _____

8. What is the main vegetation on most of the northern coast? _____

Understanding Population Maps

Population maps show where people live in an area and how many people live there.

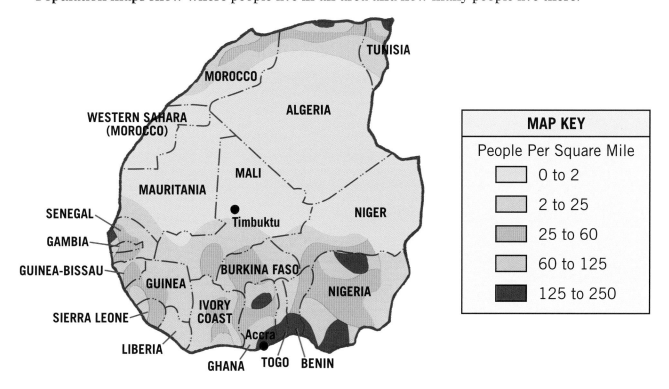

MAP KEY

People Per Square Mile

☐	0 to 2
☐	2 to 25
☐	25 to 60
☐	60 to 125
☐	125 to 250

Study the population map of western Africa. Then answer the questions below.

1. Which country generally has fewer people per square mile, Mali or Morocco? _____

2. Are there more people per square mile around Accra or Timbuktu? _____

3. Would you consider the central part of the area shown lightly settled or densely settled?

   _____

4. What is the number of people per square mile in the band of population that runs from

   Morocco to Tunisia? _____

5. In what four countries along the southern coast is the population 125 to 250 people per

   square mile? _____

6. What country has 0 to 2 people per square mile across its entire territory? _____

7. How many different categories of population does Tunisia have? _____

8. How many different categories of population does Niger have? _____

9. What are the different categories in Niger? _____

10. How many people per square mile does Liberia have? _____

Understanding Transportation Maps

Transportation maps show the routes that different types of transportation may follow. A transportation map may show train routes, bus routes, or airline routes. The map below shows the routes flown by an airline in the United States. Each line represents a flight between two cities. A flight with no stops in between is a direct flight.

Study the map. Then circle T (true) or F (false) for each statement below.

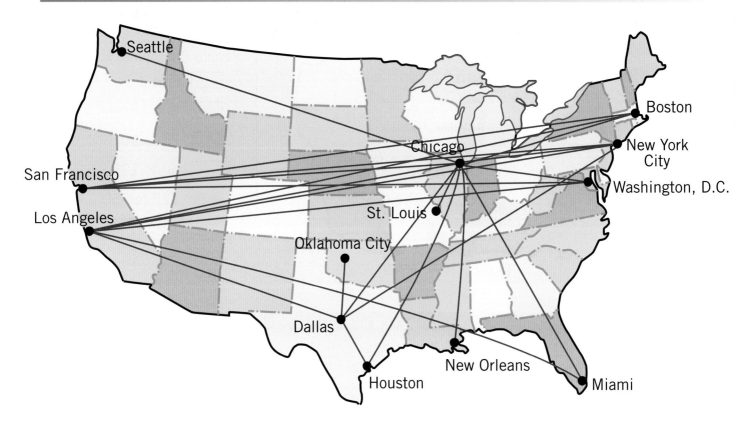

T   F   **1.** There is a direct flight between Dallas and Boston.

T   F   **2.** To fly from San Francisco to New Orleans, you have to fly to Chicago first.

T   F   **3.** There is a direct flight from Boston to Seattle.

T   F   **4.** To fly from New York to Oklahoma City, you can fly to Chicago, then to Dallas, and then to Oklahoma City.

T   F   **5.** There is a direct flight between Miami and Chicago.

T   F   **6.** There is a direct flight from Dallas to St. Louis.

T   F   **7.** To fly from Washington to San Francisco, you have to fly through Chicago.

T   F   **8.** There is a direct flight from Miami to Los Angeles.

T   F   **9.** You need to take two flights to fly from Seattle to New Orleans.

T   F   **10.** There is a direct flight from Dallas to Houston.

Understanding Weather and Transit Maps

People use **weather maps** and **transit maps** all the time. You see weather maps in newspapers and on TV. A **weather map** gives information about what the weather is expected to be for that day or the next day. It tells about expected temperatures and rainfall or snowfall.

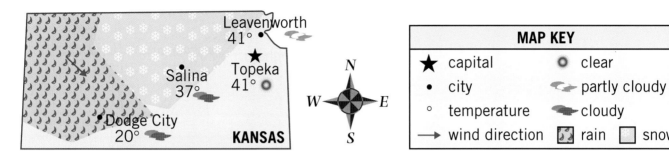

Study the weather map above and its key. Then circle T (true) or F (false) for each statement below.

T F **1.** It is snowing around Dodge City.

T F **2.** It is colder in Topeka than in Leavenworth.

T F **3.** It is snowing in Salina.

T F **4.** The wind is coming from the northwest.

T F **5.** It is cloudier in Leavenworth than in Topeka.

T F **6.** It is raining in Topeka.

A **transit map** shows how to get from one place to another on public transportation.

Study the transit map at the right and its key. Then circle T (true) or F (false) for each statement below.

T F **7.** To get from Market to Broadway on Powell, you take a cable car.

T F **8.** To get from California to Sutter on Stockton, you take the #15 bus.

T F **9.** To get from Montgomery to Powell on Market, you take the J streetcar.

T F **10.** To get from California to Columbus on Kearny, you take the #30 bus.

Using What You Have Learned

This map shows the routes flown by an airline in the United States. Each line represents a flight between two cities. Study the map. Then circle T (true) or F (false) for each statement.

T   F   **1.** You can fly directly to Birmingham from Atlanta.

T   F   **2.** To get from Orlando to Nashville, you need to fly to Atlanta.

T   F   **3.** You can fly directly from Charlotte to Birmingham.

T   F   **4.** You must go through Atlanta to fly from Miami to Charlotte.

T   F   **5.** You can fly directly from Atlanta to every city on the map.

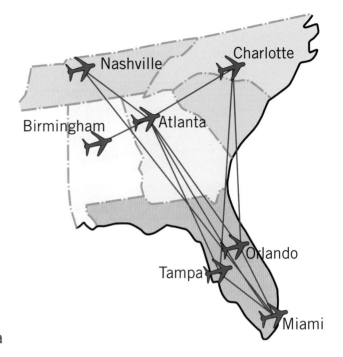

The transit map shows subway lines in New York City. Study the map. Then circle T (true) or F (false) for each statement.

T   F   **6.** All trains have an 86th Street stop.

T   F   **7.** The 1 and 9 trains end at Columbus Circle.

T   F   **8.** The 4, B, and D trains stop at 161st Street.

T   F   **9.** All trains stop at Kingsbridge Road.

T   F   **10.** The 4 train ends at Woodlawn.

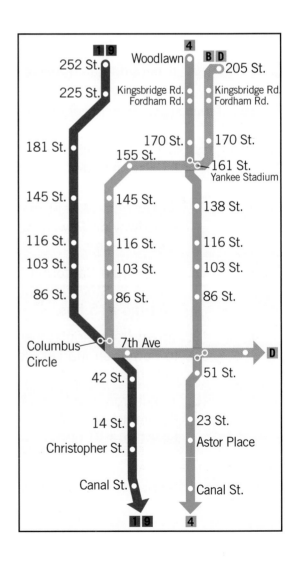

Understanding Historical Maps

Historical maps may show many different kinds of information about the past. A historical map may show where battles in a war were fought or where different people settled. The historical map below shows how boundary lines for the United States have changed over time. These changes came about because of war, revolution, purchases, or agreements.

Study this historical map of the growth of the continental United States. Then answer the questions.

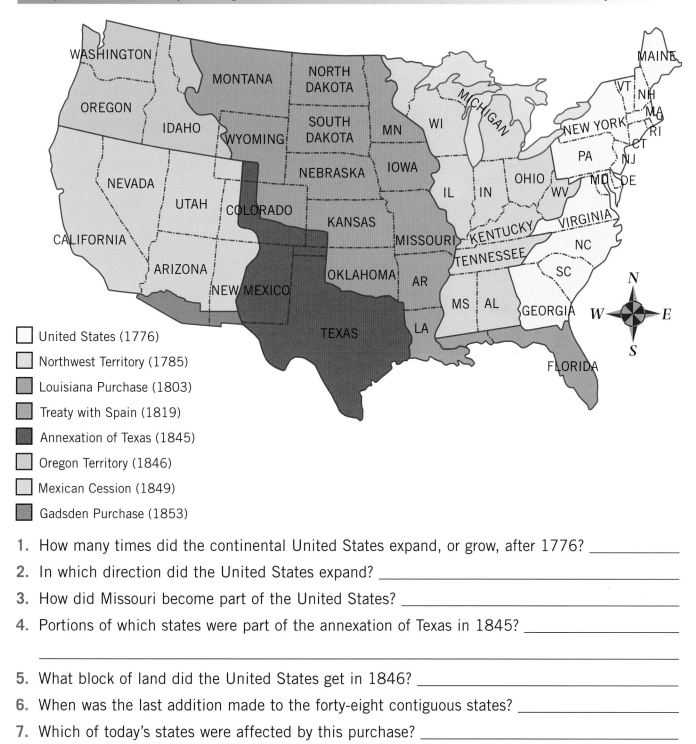

1. How many times did the continental United States expand, or grow, after 1776? _____

2. In which direction did the United States expand? _____

3. How did Missouri become part of the United States? _____

4. Portions of which states were part of the annexation of Texas in 1845? _____

_____

5. What block of land did the United States get in 1846? _____

6. When was the last addition made to the forty-eight contiguous states? _____

7. Which of today's states were affected by this purchase? _____

Understanding Language Maps

Almost anything that involves location can be mapped. The map below is a **language map.** It shows the main languages spoken in southwestern Europe.

Study the map. Then circle T (true) or F (false) for each statement below.

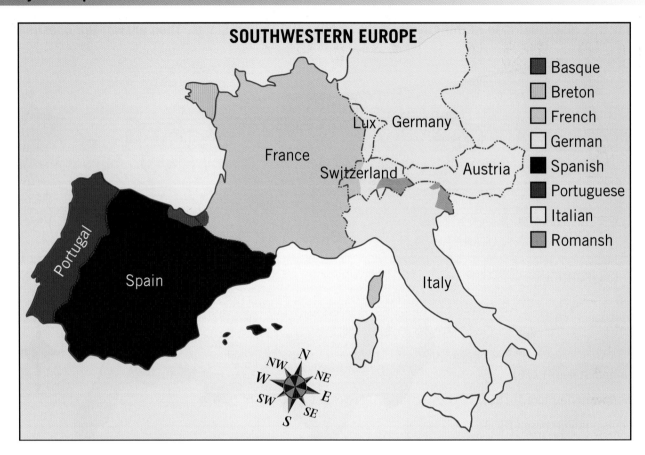

T   F   1. French is spoken in France and in part of Switzerland.

T   F   2. German is spoken only in Germany.

T   F   3. Portuguese is the main language of Spain.

T   F   4. Basque is spoken in parts of France and Spain.

T   F   5. French is the only language spoken in France.

Use the map to answer the questions below.

6. What is the main language of Italy? _____

7. What language is spoken in Austria? _____

8. What is the main language of Portugal? _____

9. What two languages are spoken in Spain? _____

10. What are the four main languages of Switzerland? _____

_____

Understanding a Map of a Recreation Area

Just about anything that shows the placement of things can be mapped. This map shows a recreation area. The recreation area has many different places where people can play different sports or do different activities.

Study the map and its key. Then answer the questions below.

1. How many different activities are shown on the map? _____

2. How many places are there for water activities? _____

3. How many baseball fields are there? _____

4. What two facilities are closest to the parking lot? _____

5. Which facilities are closer to each other, baseball and boating or swimming and tennis?

_____

6. Sixteen soccer teams arrive to play in a tournament. Two teams play in each game. How

   many teams can play soccer at the same time? _____

7. What facilities are inside the hiking trail? _____

8. What two facilities are the farthest away from the parking lot? _____

9. If a tennis player hits a shot wildly, would the ball be more likely to end up on the hiking

   trail or in the picnic area? _____

10. If a baseball player hits a home run, would it be more likely to end up on a soccer field or a

    tennis court? _____

Using What You Have Learned

Study these three maps. Then answer the questions below.

Map A

1. What year was South Carolina settled?

   _____

2. Which colony was settled first?

   _____

3. Which was the last colony settled?

   _____

4. When was Maryland settled?

   _____

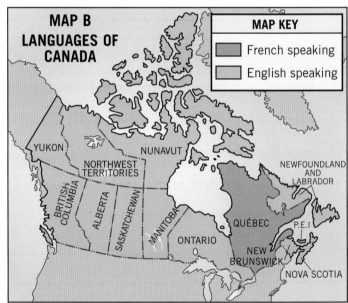

Map B

5. What language is spoken in Ontario?

   _____

6. What language is spoken in Québec?

   _____

7. What language is spoken in Nova Scotia?

   _____

Map C

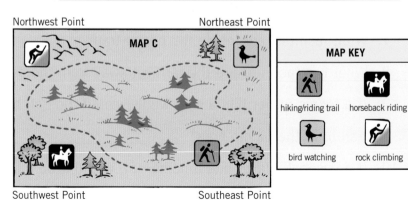

8. How many activities are shown on the map? _____

9. Does this recreation map show facilities for horseback riding or ice hockey? _____

10. What point is best for bird watching? _____

26

Map Review

_____ 1. the capital of Zambia

_____ 2. the distance from Dallas, Texas, to Fort Worth along Route 20

_____ 3. if rain is expected in your town tomorrow

_____ 4. whether Central America is usually hot or cold

_____ 5. where coal is mined in Pennsylvania

_____ 6. which subway to take in New York City

_____ 7. whether northern or southern Africa gets more rain

_____ 8. whether New Jersey or Wyoming is more densely settled

_____ 9. the highest point in Oregon

_____ 10. what language is spoken in Brazil

_____ 11. which nation ruled Poland in 1810

a. weather map
b. political map
c. land use map
d. road map
e. population map
f. climate map
g. transit map
h. rainfall map
i. historical map
j. topographic map
k. language map

Here are some map terms you should know. Beside each term, write the letter of the definition below that explains what it means.

_____ 12. key

_____ 13. scale

_____ 14. grid

_____ 15. capital

_____ 16. peninsula

_____ 17. strait

_____ 18. bay

_____ 19. elevation

_____ 20. boundary

a. a narrow body of water connecting two larger bodies of water

b. tells what the distances on a map are equal to on the ground

c. a body of water smaller than an ocean or a sea that reaches into land

d. tells what the symbols used on a map mean

e. a line separating areas under different governments

f. a large body of land surrounded by water on three sides

g. the height of an area above sea level

h. divides a map into small spaces to make it easy to find places

i. the city where the government of an area is located

Recognizing the Hemispheres on a Globe

A **globe** is a round model of Earth. Because it is shaped like a ball, a globe is the most accurate "map" of Earth that we have.

A globe shows several important imaginary points and lines on Earth. The points farthest north and south are called the **North Pole** and the **South Pole.** Halfway between them is a line

around Earth called the **equator.** It divides the globe into two halves, the **Northern Hemisphere** and the **Southern Hemisphere.** Earth can also be divided into halves by grouping the continents into the **Eastern Hemisphere** and the **Western Hemisphere.**

Western Hemisphere

Eastern Hemisphere

Study the globe drawings above. Then answer these questions.

1. What are the points farthest north and south on Earth? _____

   _____

2. What imaginary line circles Earth halfway between those points? _____

3. In which two hemispheres is North America? _____

   _____

4. In which two hemispheres is Europe? _____

   _____

5. In which three hemispheres is South America? _____

   _____

6. In which three hemispheres is Africa? _____

   _____

7. In which three hemispheres is Antarctica? _____

   _____

Understanding Latitude and Longitude

The lines running east-west around a globe are called **latitude lines,** or **parallels.** They mark distances north and south of the equator in **degrees** (°). Degrees can be divided into smaller units called **minutes** (´), so 66°30´ is read 66 degrees 30 minutes. There are 60 minutes in a degree.

There are some special parallels: the equator at 0°, the Tropic of Cancer at 23°30´ N, the Arctic Circle at 66°30´ N, the North Pole at 90° N, the Tropic of Capricorn at 23°30´ S, the Antarctic Circle at 66°30´ S, and the South Pole at 90° S.

The lines running north-south around a globe are called **longitude lines,** or **meridians.** They mark the distances in degrees east and west of the **prime meridian,** which is at 0°.

Using the two sets of lines together as a grid, you can easily find any place on a globe. If a point X is at 20° S, 20° E, you just look across the latitude line at 20 degrees south of the equator and down the longitude line at 20 degrees east of the prime meridian to find it.

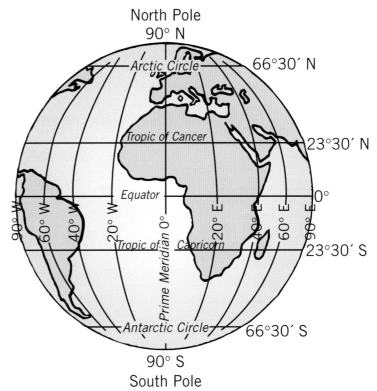

Study the globe drawing above. Then answer the questions below.

1. What latitude line is 0°? _____

2. What longitude line is 0°? _____

3. At what latitude is the North Pole? _____ The South Pole? _____

4. What special parallel is at 23°30´ N? _____

   At 23°30´ S? _____

5. What special parallel is at 66°30´ N? _____

   At 66°30´ S? _____

6. What distances do latitude lines mark? _____

   _____

7. What distances do longitude lines mark? _____

   _____

Using Latitude and Longitude

The map below shows how the countries in and around the Middle East look on a globe.

Study the map. Then answer these questions.

1. Between which two latitude lines is Iran located?

   _____

   _____

2. Between which two longitude lines is Saudi Arabia located?

   _____

   _____

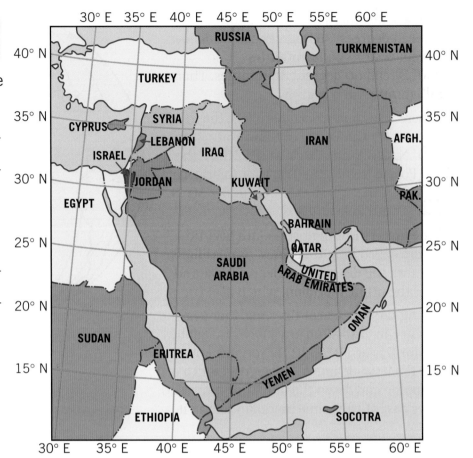

Find each grid location listed below on the map. Then write the letter of the country in which the grid location lies.

3. 30° N, 45° E _____

4. 40° N, 35° E _____

5. 25° N, 30° E _____

6. 20° N, 35° E _____

7. 35° N, 40° E _____

8. 20° N, 50° E _____

9. 30° N, 55° E _____

10. 30° N, 35° E _____

a. Egypt

b. Syria

c. Iraq

d. Iran

e. Turkey

f. Sudan

g. Saudi Arabia

h. Israel

Understanding Time Zones

Earth rotates, or turns, on its **axis,** an imaginary line that runs through its center from the North Pole to the South Pole. It makes one complete turn every 24 hours, which creates sunrises and sunsets at different times in different places. To make keeping time easier, most of the world's countries have agreed on **standard time zones.** Each zone covers about 15° longitude and is an hour earlier as you move west. The **International Date Line,** most of which runs along the longitude line at 180°, marks the beginning of each new day. So when you cross this line going west, you gain a day. When you cross it going east, you lose a day. In other words, if it is Saturday on the east side of the International Date Line, it is Friday on the west side.

This map shows some of the world's time zones. Use the map to answer the questions below.

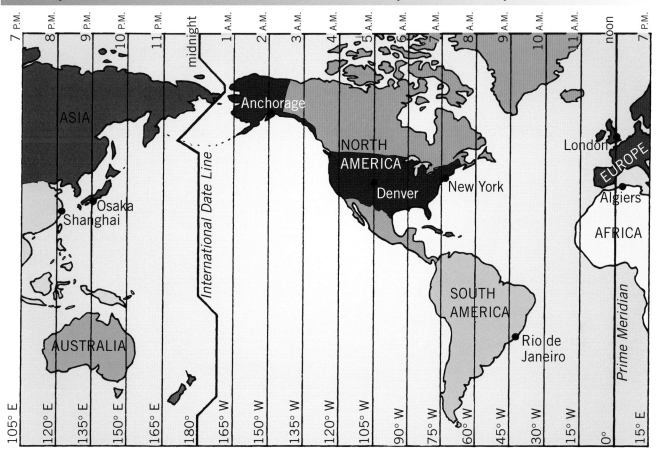

1. At what longitude is most of the International Date Line? _____

2. If it is midnight along the International Date Line, what time is it along the prime meridian?

   _____

3. If it is Tuesday in Shanghai, China, what day is it in Anchorage, Alaska? _____

4. If it is 7 A.M. in New York City, what time is it in London, England? _____

   In Denver, Colorado? _____

5. If it is 2 A.M. in Shanghai, China, what time is it in Osaka, Japan? _____

6. If it is 3 A.M. in Denver, Colorado, what time is it in Rio de Janeiro, Brazil? _____

   In Algiers in Africa? _____ In Anchorage, Alaska? _____

31

Globe Review

On the drawing of the globe below, label these important points and lines. Then answer the questions below.

1. North Pole
2. South Pole
3. Equator

4. Tropic of Cancer
5. Tropic of Capricorn
6. Arctic Circle

7. Antarctic Circle
8. Prime Meridian

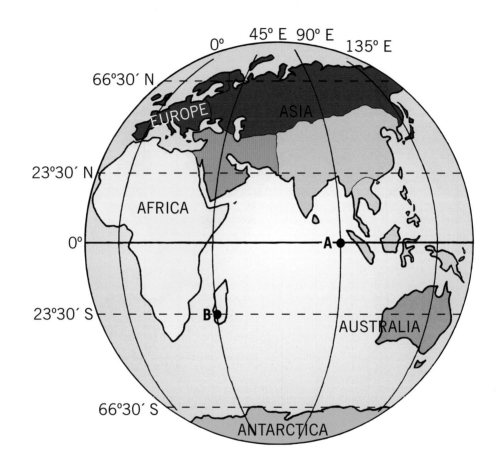

9. What three hemispheres are visible on the globe drawing? _____

_____

10. Is the equator a latitude or longitude line? _____

11. Is the prime meridian a latitude or longitude line? _____

12. What is the grid designation of point A on the drawing? _____

    Of point B? _____

13. If it is 3 P.M. in Algiers (Africa), is it 11 P.M. or 7 A.M. in Shanghai (Asia)? _____

14. If it is 6 A.M. in Denver, Colorado, is it 4 A.M. or 8 A.M. in New York? _____

Globe Review

1. Find the location of each of these cities on the map. Mark the location with a dot and write the city's name next to it.
   A. Managua (12° N, 86° W)
   B. Havana (23° N, 82° W)
   C. Mexico City (19° N, 99° W)
   D. Caracas (11° N, 67° W)

2. The Panama Canal lies at about 9° N, 80° W. Label it on the map.

3. Label the islands of Jamaica (17° N, 77° W) and Puerto Rico (18° N, 67° W). Label Lake Maracaibo (10° N, 72° W). Label Mount Chimborazo (2° S, 78° W).

Write the name of the country in which you find each of the following places.

4. Tabasco (18° N, 98° W) _____

5. Cali (3° N, 77° W) _____

6. Cartago (10° N, 84° W) _____

7. Santo Domingo (18° N, 70° W) _____

Understanding Map Projections

A flat map of the world cannot show Earth as accurately as a globe. But mapmakers do use views of Earth, called **projections,** which show at least part of Earth accurately. Each kind of projection serves a different purpose.

A **Mercator projection** uses straight lines for both latitude and longitude. Because of this, size and distance are accurate only along the equator. Toward the poles, things on the map become more distorted, or inaccurate. However, a Mercator projection does show the correct shape of land areas and true direction. So these maps are very useful for sailors setting their course by a compass.

In order to show the sizes and shapes of certain land and water areas as accurately as a globe, mapmakers have to add blank space to their flat map. This kind of map plan is known as an **interrupted projection.** As you can see, distances and directions are hard to figure out on an interrupted projection.

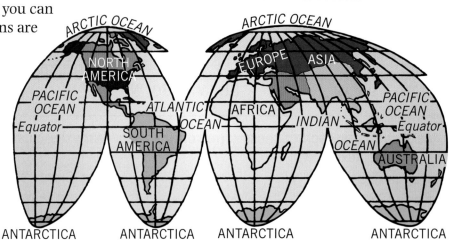

MERCATOR PROJECTION

INTERRUPTED PROJECTION

Study the map projections above. Then answer these questions.

1. Which projection best shows true direction? _____

2. Which projection best shows true size? _____

3. Which projection has straight longitude lines? _____

4. Which projection is most useful for sailors? _____

5. Which projection splits land and water areas with blank space? _____

Understanding the Robinson Map Projection

Mapmakers have the problem of how to show a round world on a flat surface. Every map projection has some advantages but also some disadvantages. The Mercator projection distorts the world at the poles so that Greenland seems much larger than it actually is. The interrupted projection makes it difficult to figure distances and direction.

Many atlases use the **Robinson projection.** The advantage of the Robinson projection is that it shows Earth more as it really appears. Lines of longitude are curved as they are on a globe. The continents appear closer to their true shape. The areas around the poles are flattened somewhat, but not distorted as much as on the Mercator projection. The distances are not quite accurate though.

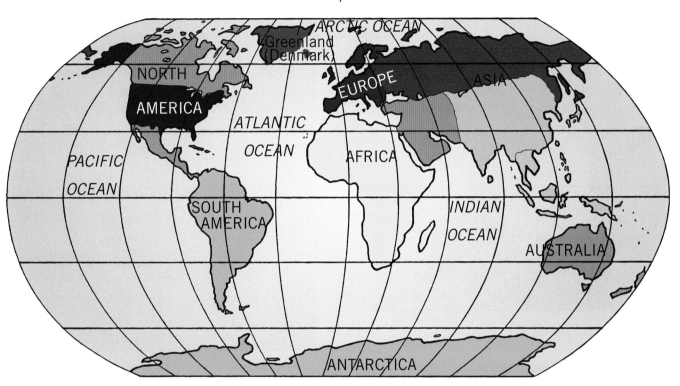

Study the Robinson projection. Then read the sentences below. Circle T if the sentence is true or F if it is false.

T   F   **1.** Lines of latitude are straight on the Robinson projection.

T   F   **2.** Lines of longitude are curved on the Robinson projection.

T   F   **3.** Greenland is badly distorted on the Robinson projection.

T   F   **4.** The Robinson projection shows almost the true shape of continents.

T   F   **5.** The Robinson projection does not distort the poles at all.

T   F   **6.** The Robinson projection shows the middle latitudes more accurately than the polar areas.

T   F   **7.** Africa is more distorted than Australia.

T   F   **8.** The Robinson projection shows the Pacific Ocean without any interruption, just as it appears on a globe.

Understanding Polar Map Projections

Another kind of map plan is called a **polar projection** because it shows Earth from one of the two poles. On a polar projection, latitude lines are shown as circles. Longitude lines are shown as straight lines through the poles. On polar projections, size and shape are most accurate near the poles and more distorted toward the edges of the maps. However, since polar projections show true distance, they are very useful for pilots. A straight line drawn from point to point will be the shortest flying route.

A polar projection that shows Earth from the North pole is called a **North Polar projection.** On this kind of map, north is the direction toward the center. A polar projection that shows Earth from the South Pole is called a **South Polar projection.** On this kind of map, the direction toward the center is south.

NORTH POLAR
PROJECTION

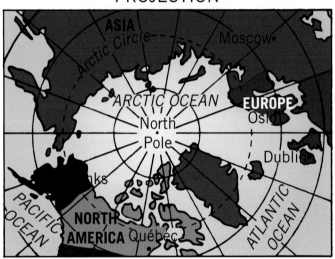

SOUTH POLAR
PROJECTION

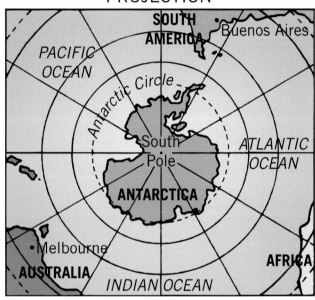

Study the polar projections. Then answer these questions.

1. Why are polar projections useful for pilots? _____

_____

2. What three continents are shown on the North Polar projection? _____

_____

3. Is Australia north or south of Antarctica? _____

4. Is Dublin, Ireland, north or south of Oslo, Norway? _____

Draw a line to show the shortest air route between each of these pairs of cities:

5. Moscow to Québec

6. Fairbanks to Dublin

7. Oslo to Moscow

8. Melbourne to Buenos Aires

Understanding Great Circle Routes

If you were a pilot going from New York to Beijing, China, in what direction would you fly? If you were looking at a Mercator projection, you might think that you should fly directly west. But on a polar projection, you can see that the shortest route from New York to Beijing would take you north, toward the North Pole.

The most direct route between two places on Earth is called a **great circle route.** Pilots use these routes because they are the quickest way to fly from one place to another.

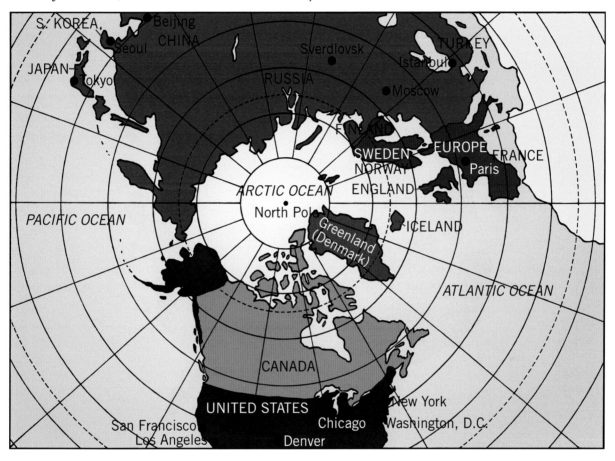

Study the North Polar projection above. Then draw a straight line, or a great circle route, on the map between each of these pairs of cities.

1. Los Angeles to Tokyo, Japan
2. Chicago to Istanbul, Turkey
3. New York to Seoul, South Korea

4. San Francisco to Sverdlovsk, Russia
5. Denver to Paris, France

Suppose the president of Russia is flying from Moscow to Washington, D.C. Draw a great circle route between those two cities. What five countries, other than the United States and Russia, does that route cross?

Understanding Lambert's Map Projection

A **Lambert's projection** is also a useful map plan for pilots because, like a polar projection, it shows the shortest flying route between places.

A Lambert's projection is also called a **conic projection.** If a cone were placed over a globe, it would touch the globe at two parallels. A map made of the area between these parallels will be accurate in distance, direction, size, and shape between the middle latitudes. North or south of these parallels, however, everything is distorted.

On a Lambert's projection, the parallels are drawn as curving lines. The meridians are drawn as if they were coming down from the top of a cone. The map below shows the United States (except Alaska and Hawaii) on a Lambert's projection.

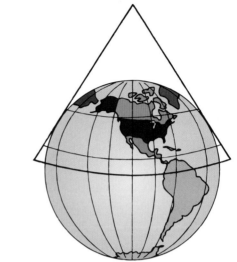

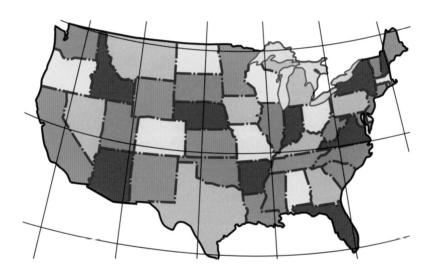

Read each sentence below. Write T if the sentence is true or F if it is false.

_____ 1. Between the middle latitudes touched by the cone, a Lambert's projection shows true size and distance.

_____ 2. It does not, however, show true direction and shape.

_____ 3. A Lambert's projection is equally accurate north and south of those parallels.

_____ 4. A Lambert's projection is useful for pilots.

_____ 5. On a Lambert's projection, parallels are straight lines.

_____ 6. On a Lambert's projection, meridians are drawn as if they were coming down from a cone.

_____ 7. On a Lambert's projection, the meridians and parallels do not cross.

Map Projection Review

Look at these five map projections. Label each one: Mercator projection, Robinson projection, South Polar projection, interrupted projection, Lambert's projection. Then answer the questions below.

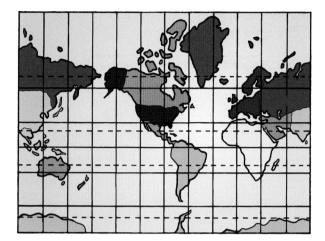

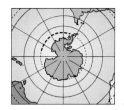

_____

_____

_____

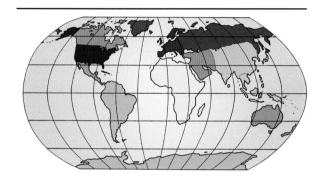

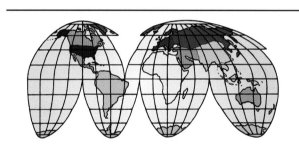

_____

_____

1. On which projection are latitude lines only slightly curved? _____

2. Which projection would be most useful for a pilot flying from Australia to Brazil?

   _____

3. Which map on the page shows land and water areas most accurately? _____

4. What are the disadvantages of a Mercator projection? _____

   _____

5. What are the advantages of a Robinson projection? _____

   _____

6. If you were a pilot, would you use an interrupted projection or a Lambert's projection? Why?

   _____

   _____

Understanding Different Types of Atlases

An **atlas** is a book of maps and may contain many different types of maps. In addition to political and physical maps, a geographic atlas may contain some or all of the following **special purpose maps:** climate, rainfall, population, vegetation, land use, and topographic. A historical atlas contains maps that show historical events, such as battles or where people settled or how the government of an area changed over time.

Physical Map

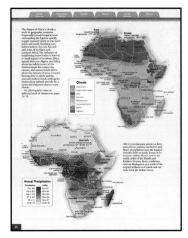

Climate and
Rainfall Maps

Read each item below. Then write G if you would find the information in a geographic atlas or H if you would find the answer in a historical atlas.

_____ 1. lands controlled by the British Empire in 1900

_____ 2. the Battle of Saratoga in the American Revolution

_____ 3. a rainfall map of Indonesia

_____ 4. population map of Egypt

_____ 5. population map of Egypt in 1790

_____ 6. Native Americans in the Southwest in 1800

_____ 7. a land use map of California

_____ 8. land controlled by the Inca Empire in South America

_____ 9. a physical map of Central America

_____ 10. major cities in modern Southeast Asia

_____ 11. routes taken by Columbus and other European explorers

_____ 12. a topographic map of Mount Everest

_____ 13. independent nations in Africa in 1960

Understanding the Index in an Atlas

An **atlas** is a book of maps, but there are different kinds of atlases. The best way to find information in an atlas is to use the **index**, a listing of the items contained in a book. In an atlas, the index usually lists places in alphabetical order followed by the page number of the map on which the place appears. The entry may also list the latitude and longitude coordinates to help you find the place on the map. Places like lakes and gulfs are usually listed by the place name first, for example *Superior, Lake.*

Place	Page	Latitude	Longitude
O			
Omaha, *NE*	**51**	41°16′ N	95°56′ W
Oman, *country*	**96**	19°00′ N	55°00′ E
Oman, G. of, *gulf*	**97**	24°00′ N	60°00′ E
Omsk, *Russia*	**96**	55°01′ N	73°20′ E
Onitsha, *Nigeria*	**90**	6°08′ N	6°47′ E
Ontario, *province, Canada*	**74**	52°00′ N	88°00′ W
Ontario, L., *lake*	**45**	45°00′ N	78°00′ W
Orange, *river*	**91**	28°00′ S	20°00′ E
Oregon, *state, U.S.*	**50**	44°00′ N	121°00′ W

Study this portion of a sample atlas index. Then complete the sentences.

1. Oregon can be found on page _____.

2. The coordinates for Oman are _____.

3. What are the page number and the coordinates for the Gulf of Oman? _____

4. What are the page number and the coordinates for Onitsha, Nigeria? _____

5. To find Mount Everest in the index, what letter would you look under? _____

6. To find the Gulf of St. Lawrence in the index, what letter would you look under? _____

Atlases also contain tables of information that list and compare geographic facts.

Study this sample atlas table. Then answer the questions below.

Country	Area (in sq. miles)	Population (2002)	Pop. per Sq. Mile
Belgium	11,779	10,275,000	872
Italy	116, 303	57,716,000	496
Sweden	173,731	8,877,000	51

7. Which country has the smallest population? _____ The largest area?

_____ The most people per square mile? _____

Understanding the Index in an Atlas

Study this sample atlas page. Then complete the sample atlas index by filling in the blanks. The first one has been done for you.

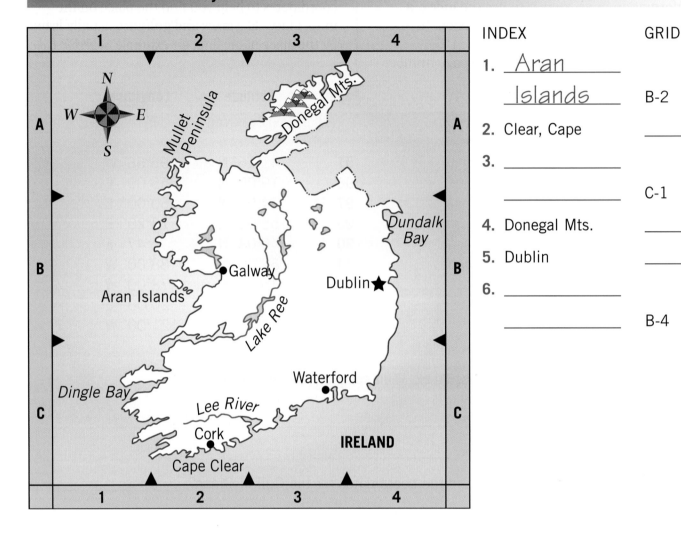

INDEX	GRID
1. _Aran Islands_	B-2
2. Clear, Cape	_____
3. _____	C-1
4. Donegal Mts.	_____
5. Dublin	_____
6. _____	B-4

Different atlases may have different kinds of indexes. The index on this page gives map coordinates rather than latitude and longitude coordinates.

Use the grid coordinates to find the following places on the map. Write the grid coordinates below.

7. Mullet Peninsula   _____

8. Cork   _____

9. Waterford   _____

10. Galway   _____

11. Lee, River   _____

12. Ree, Lake   _____

Finding Special Purpose Maps in an Atlas

Geographic atlases contain special purpose maps about such topics as climate, rainfall, population, vegetation, transportation, land use, and language. An historical atlas will contain maps about past events.

The items below are about the United States. On each line write the type of map on which you would find the information. Then use a classroom atlas to find the page number of each map and write it on the line.

1. the most densely settled area in Utah _____

_____

2. a manufacturing area in Illinois _____

_____

3. a coal mining area in West Virginia _____

_____

4. a climate region of California _____

_____

5. the average rainfall in western Texas _____

_____

6. a desert in the United States _____

_____

7. a major airport in California _____

_____

8. the location of forests in Florida _____

_____

9. a gold mining area in the United States _____

_____

10. a major road in the Northeast _____

_____

11. the average rainfall in the Great Plains _____

_____

12. the population along the U.S. coast of the Gulf of Mexico _____

_____

Finding Special Purpose Maps in an Atlas

1. a country with a rain forest _____

_____

2. the location of most of the marine climate zones _____

_____

3. a country with gold mining _____

_____

4. a country with the lowest amount of rainfall _____

_____

5. a major population center _____

_____

6. a country with grasslands _____

_____

7. the average rainfall in Uruguay _____

_____

8. the population in the Amazon Basin _____

_____

9. the main climate zone of Brazil _____

_____

10. the population in Quito, Ecuador _____

_____

11. the vegetation along the western part of Peru _____

_____

12. a coal-producing country _____

_____

Finding Special Purpose Maps in an Atlas

The items below are about the Eastern Hemisphere. On each line write the type of map on which you would find the information. Then use a classroom atlas to find the information or name of a place. Write the answer and the page number of each map on the line.

1. the location of oil wells in India _____

_____

2. the greatest population area of China _____

_____

3. a country in Africa with desert vegetation _____

_____

4. the average rainfall in southern Italy _____

_____

5. an area of marine climate in Europe _____

_____

6. a desert in Central Asia _____

_____

7. the average precipitation in Sri Lanka _____

_____

8. the population of Iran _____

_____

9. a country in Africa with a rain forest _____

_____

10. a tundra region in Russia _____

_____

11. a city near a coal mining area in Japan _____

_____

12. the population along the Arctic coast of Russia _____

_____

Atlas Review

The facts below can all be found in geographic atlases. Use an atlas to find the answer to each question.

1. What river forms the boundary between Canada and part of New York State?

   _____

2. What country stretches across part of Europe and all of Asia to the Pacific Ocean?

   _____

3. Which of the following cities in Brazil is located inland along the Amazon River: Recife,

   São Paolo, or Manaus? _____

4. Which of the following African countries is mostly desert: Libya, Tanzania, or Nigeria?

   _____

5. Does the middle of Australia have an arid climate or a mediterranean climate?

   _____

6. What is the capital of Spain? _____

7. Which of the following African countries has oil resources: Sudan, Somalia, or Nigeria?

   _____

8. What countries border Paraguay in South America? _____

9. What mountain range runs along the border between France and Spain?

   _____

10. What is the tallest mountain in Japan? _____

11. Which country in Asia gets more rainfall, Mongolia or Malaysia?

   _____

12. The Red Sea separates which two continents? _____

13. What is the name of the peninsula that is part of Mexico and extends south from California?

   _____

14. What body of water forms the coast of Kenya? _____

15. Which city is larger in population, Chicago, Illinois, or New Orleans, Louisiana?

   _____

Glossary

archipelago	a group of islands
Antarctic Circle	a line of latitude at 66°30′ S
Arctic Circle	a line of latitude at 66°30′ N
atlas	a book of maps
axis	an imaginary line that runs through the center of Earth
bay	a small area of ocean or sea that reaches into the land
boundary line	a line that marks the place where one area ends and another begins
cape	a small, pointed peninsula
capital	the city in a state or country where the government is located
climate map	a map that shows the overall weather of different areas
compass rose	a set of arrows that shows direction; direction finder
conic projection	another name for Lambert's projection
continent	one of the seven largest bodies of land on Earth
degrees	how lines of latitude and longitude are measured
delta	the build-up of mud and sand at the mouth of a river
direction finder	a set of arrows that shows direction
downstream	the direction a river flows
Eastern Hemisphere	the eastern half of the globe
elevation	height above sea level
globe	a round model of Earth that is tilted and turns just as Earth does
great circle route	the most direct route between two places on Earth
grid	lines dividing a map to help you find places
gulf	a large body of water reaching into land from an ocean or sea
historical map	a map that shows political boundaries or land use at a point in the past
index	an alphabetical list of subjects in a book
International Date Line	an imaginary line that runs mostly along longitude line 180° marking the boundary between one day and the next
interrupted projection	a map projection that shows land and some water areas accurately, but leaves spaces in the map to do so
island	land completely surrounded by water
isthmus	a narrow strip of land that connects two larger areas of land
key	an explanation of the symbols used on a map
lake	an inland body of water
Lambert's projection	a map projection featuring curved parallels and meridians drawn as if they were coming down from the top of a cone
land use map	a map that shows where things are grown, raised, mined, and made
language map	a map that shows which languages are spoken in certain areas
latitude line	an imaginary line that encircles the globe from left to right
longitude line	an imaginary line that encircles the globe from top to bottom
map	a drawing of a place as you would see it from above
Mercator projection	a map of Earth with straight lines of latitude and longitude

Glossary

meridian	a line of longitude
mileage marker	a point on a map that shows the mileage between two places
mileage table	a chart of distances between places
minute	one-sixtieth of a degree
mouth	where a river flows into a larger body of water
natural features	bodies of land and bodies of water on Earth
Northern Hemisphere	the northern half of the globe
North Polar projection	a map of Earth from the North Pole
North Pole	the point farthest north on Earth
ocean	one of the four largest areas of water on Earth
parallel	a line of latitude
peninsula	land surrounded by water on three sides
polar climate	cold climate zone found near the poles
polar projection	a map that shows Earth from one of the two poles
political map	a map that shows areas under different governments
population map	a map that shows the number of people living in an area
prime meridian	a line of longitude at 0° that runs through Greenwich, England
projections	how mapmakers show round Earth on a flat map
rainfall map	a map that shows how much rain falls in different places over time
river	a long body of water that flows along a certain path
road map	a map that shows roads and distances
Robinson projection	a map of Earth with curved lines of longitude
scale	shows distance on a map
sea	a large body of water smaller than an ocean
source	where a river begins
Southern Hemisphere	the southern half of the globe
South Polar projection	a map of Earth from the South Pole
South Pole	the point farthest south on Earth
special purpose map	a map that shows specialized information such as rainfall
standard time zones	15° of longitude and an hour apart
strait	a narrow body of water that connects two larger bodies of water
street map	a detailed road map that shows the streets of a city
temperate climate	mild climate zone between the Tropic of Cancer and the Arctic Circle and the Tropic of Capricorn and the Antarctic Circle
topographic map	a map that shows the elevation of an area
transit map	a map that shows how to get from one place to another on public transportation
tributary	a river that runs into a larger river
tropical climate	hot climate zone found between the Tropic of Cancer and the Tropic of Capricorn
Tropic of Cancer	a line of latitude at 23°30´ N
Tropic of Capricorn	a line of latitude at 23°30´ S
vegetation map	a map that shows the plant life in an area
Western Hemisphere	the western half of the globe